▌▌SCHOLASTIC

Informational Passages
for Text Marking & Close Reading

GRADE **4**

By Marcia Miller & Martin Lee

NEW YORK • TORONTO • LONDON • AUCKLAND • SYDNEY
MEXICO CITY • NEW DELHI • HONG KONG • BUENOS AIRES

Teaching *Resources*

Cover design: Brian LaRossa
Interior design: Kathy Massaro

Photos © 14: Avava/iStockphoto; 16: Courtesy of Aprilli Design Studio; 18: MTomczak/Bigstock; 20: njnightsky/iStockphoto; 26 top: Mathew Hayward/123RF; 26 bottom: Elenathewise/Thinkstock; 28 top: Valerii Zan/Dreamstime; 28 bottom: vvoe/Shutterstock, Inc.; 30: Jktu_21/Shutterstock, Inc.; 32: spinetta/Shutterstock, Inc.; 34: Ingram_Publishing/iStockphoto; 36: Sadeugra/iStockphoto; 38: Peter Gudella/Shutterstock, Inc.; 40: Ivonne Wierink/Shutterstock, Inc.; 42: Courtesy of Dave Soldier; 44: Courtesy of LucasFilms; 46: Tribalium/Shutterstock, Inc.; 48: Debby Wong/Shutterstock, Inc.; 50: anawat sudchanham/Shutterstock, Inc.; 52: Gene J. Puskar/AP Images.

ISBN: 978-0-545-79380-3
Copyright © 2015 by Scholastic Inc.
All rights reserved.
Printed in the U.S.A.
Published by Scholastic Inc.

4 5 6 7 8 9 10   40   22 21 20 19 18 17

Contents

Informational Text Passages

Main Idea & Details

Sequence of Events

Fact & Opinion

Compare & Contrast

Cause & Effect

Context Clues

Problem & Solution

Summarize

Make inferences

Author's Purpose

Introduction

The vast majority of what adults read—in books, magazines, or online—is nonfiction. We read news stories, memoirs, science pieces, sports articles, business e-mails and memos, editorials, arts reviews, health documents, assembly or installation instructions, advertisements, and catalogs. Informational reading, with its diverse structures, formats, and content-specific vocabulary, can be demanding.

Many students enjoy reading nonfiction, but navigating the wide variety of rich informational texts poses challenges for evolving readers. Students may lack sufficient background knowledge of a topic or be unfamiliar with specific vocabulary related to it. In addition, they may find some structures or features of nonfiction puzzling. This is why exposing students more frequently to complex informational texts and introducing them to active reading-comprehension strategies are now key components of successful reading instruction. Useful strategies, clearly taught, can empower readers to approach informational texts purposefully, closely, and independently. Such active tools provide students with a foundation for success not only in school, but for the rest of their lives.

> **Connections to the Standards**
>
> The chart on page 9 details how the lessons in this book will help your students meet the more rigorous demands of today's reading standards for informational text.

Text Marking: A Powerful Active-Reading Strategy

To improve their comprehension of complex informational texts, students must actively engage with the text. Careful and consistent text marking by hand is one valuable way to accomplish that. To begin with, by numbering paragraphs, students can readily identify the location of pertinent information when discussing a piece. By circling main ideas, underlining supporting details (such as definitions, descriptions, evidence, explanations, and data), and boxing key vocabulary, students interact directly with the material, making it more digestible in the process. But the true goal of teaching text marking is to help students internalize an effective close-reading strategy, not to have them show how many marks they can make on a page.

Purposeful text marking intensifies a reader's focus. It helps readers identify information as they read and recognize and isolate key details or connect relevant ideas presented in the text. For instance, boxing words like *before, next, finally,* and *afterwards* can clarify the sequence of ideas or events in a passage. By circling expressions like *I think* or *in my opinion,* students learn to discern opinions from facts. When students are asked to compare and contrast information in a passage, boxing signal words and phrases, such as *both, in the same way,* or *however,* can make identifying similarities and differences more apparent. Words like *since, because of, therefore,* or *as a result* signal cause-and-effect relationships that structure a piece. Furthermore, the physical act of writing by hand, in itself, helps students not only process what they read, but remember it as well.

About the Passages

The 20 reproducible passages in this book, which vary in genres and forms, organizational structures, purposes, tones, and tasks, address ten key reading-comprehension skills, from identifying main ideas and details, and separating facts from opinions to summarizing and making inferences. Consult the table of contents to see the scope of skills, genres, forms, content areas, and Lexile scores of the passages. The Lexile scores fall within the ranges recommended for fourth graders. (The scores for grade 4, revised to reflect the more rigorous demands of today's higher standards, range from 740 to 940.)

Each passage appears on its own page, beginning with the title, the genre or form of the passage, and the main comprehension skill the passage addresses. Most of the passages include visual elements, such as photographs, illustrations, or diagrams, as well as typical text elements, such as italics, boldface type, subheadings, sidebars, and captions.

The passages are stand-alone texts and can be used in any order you choose. Feel free to assign passages to individuals, pairs, small groups, or the entire class, as best suits your teaching style. However, it's a good idea to preview each passage before you assign it, to ensure that your students have the skills needed to complete it successfully. (See the next page for a close-reading routine to model for students.)

Reading-Comprehension Question Pages

Following each passage is a reproducible "Do More" page of text-dependent comprehension questions: two are multiple-choice questions that call for a single response and a brief, text-based explanation to justify that choice. The other two questions are open-response items. The questions address a range of comprehension strategies and skills. All questions share the goal of ensuring that students engage in close reading of the text, grasp its key ideas, and provide text-based evidence to support their answers. Have additional paper on hand so students have ample space to write complete and thorough answers.

An answer key (pages 54–63) includes annotated versions of each marked passage and sample answers to its related questions. Maintain flexibility in assessing student responses, as some markings and answers to open-response questions may vary. (Since students are likely to mark different places in the text as examples for particular skills, the annotated versions in the answer key highlight a variety of possible responses.) Encourage students to self-assess and revise their answers as you review the text markings together. This approach encourages discussion, comparison, extension, reinforcement, and correlation to other reading skills.

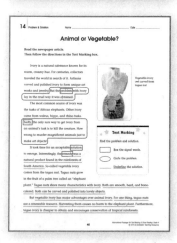

Teaching Routine for Close Reading and Purposeful Text Marking

Any text can become more accessible to readers who have learned to bring various strategies, such as purposeful text marking, to the reading process. Here is one suggested routine that may be effective in your classroom.

Preview

- **Engage prior knowledge** of the topic of the piece and its genre. Help students link it to similar topics or examples of the genre they may have read.

- **Identify the reading skill** for which students will be marking the text. Distribute the Comprehension Skill Summary Card that applies to the passage. Go over its key ideas. (See Comprehension Skill Summary Cards, page 8, for more.)

Model *(for the first passage, to familiarize students with the process)*

- **Display the passage**, using an interactive whiteboard, document camera, or other resource, and provide students with their own copy. Preview the text with students by having them read the title and look at any photographs, illustrations, or other graphics.

- **Draw attention to the markings** students will use to enhance their understanding of the piece. Link the text marking box to the Comprehension Skill Summary Card for clarification.

- **Read aloud the passage** as students follow along. Guide students to think about the skill and to note any questions they may have on sticky-notes.

- **Mark the text together.** Begin by numbering the paragraphs. Then discuss the choices you make when marking the text, demonstrating and explaining how the various text elements support the skill. Check that students understand how to mark the text using the various icons and graphics shown in the text marking box.

Read

- **Have students do a quick-read of the passage independently** for the gist. Then they should read it a second time, marking the text as they go.

- **Encourage students to make additional markings of their own.** These might include noting unfamiliar vocabulary, an idiom or phrase they may not understand, or an especially interesting, unusual, or important detail they want to remember. Invite them to use sticky-notes, colored pencils, highlighters, question marks, or check marks.

Respond

- **Have students read the passage a third time.** This reading should prepare them to discuss the piece and offer their views about it.

- **Have students answer the questions** on the companion Do More page. Encourage them to look back at their text markings and other text evidence. This will help students provide complete and supported responses.

Informational Passages for Text Marking & Close Reading: Grade 4
© 2015 by Scholastic Teaching Resources

Comprehension Skill Summary Cards

To help students review the ten reading-comprehension skills this book addresses and the specific terms associated with each, have them use the ten reproducible Comprehension Skill Summary Cards (pages 10–12). The boldface terms on each card are the same ones students will identify as they mark the text.

You might duplicate, cut out, and distribute a particular Comprehension Skill Summary Card before assigning a passage that focuses on that skill. Discuss the elements of the skill together to ensure that students fully grasp it. Encourage students to save and collect the cards, which they can use as a set of reading aids to refer to whenever they read any type of informational text.

Tips and Suggestions

- The text-marking process is versatile and adaptable. Although numbering, boxing, circling, and underlining are the most common methods, you can personalize the strategy for your class if it helps augment the process. You might have students use letters to mark text; they can, for example, write MI to indicate a main idea, D to mark a detail, or F for fact and O for opinion. Whichever technique you use, focus on the need for consistency of marking.

- You may wish to extend the text-marking strategy by having students identify other aspects of writing, such as figurative language or confusing words, expressions, or idioms. Moreover, you can invite students to write their own notes and questions in the margins.

Comprehension Skill

Main Idea & Details

Every passage has one or more main ideas supported by details. The main idea answers the question, "Who (or What) is this piece about?"

- The **main idea** is the most important point an author makes about a topic. The main idea in most paragraphs is stated in a *topic sentence*. The topic sentence can appear anywhere in a paragraph.
- **Supporting details** are facts, statements, examples, descriptions, and other information that tell more about the main idea.

Comprehension Skill

Sequence of Events

As you read, notice the order in which things happen or ideas are presented. Think about the *beginning, middle,* and *end.*

- **Events** are the important actions that happen.
- The **sequence** is the order in which events happen.
- **Signal words** give clues that help clarify the order of events. Examples include *first, second, third, next, then, last, later, before, prior to, soon, during, while, after, finally,* as well as specific dates and times.

Comprehension Skill

Compare & Contrast

Authors discuss people, places, objects, or ideas by describing how they are alike and ways they differ.

- To **compare** means to tell how two or more things are alike.
- To **contrast** means to tell how two or more things are different.
- **Signal words** guide you to compare and contrast.

Examples for comparing: *both, like, alike, also, too, share, in the same way,* and *similarly.*

Examples for contrasting: *but, only, unlike, instead, however, in contrast, different, although, on the other hand, as opposed to, neither, whereas, while,* and *rather.*

Informational Passages for Text Marking & Close Reading: Grade 4
© 2015 by Scholastic Teaching Resources

Connections to the Standards

The lessons in this book support the College and Career Readiness Anchor Standards for Reading for students in grades K–12. These broad standards, which serve as the basis of many state standards, were developed to establish rigorous educational expectations with the goal of providing students nationwide with a quality education that prepares them for college and careers. The chart below details how the lessons align with specific reading standards for informational text for students in grade 4.

These materials also address language standards, including skills in the conventions of standard English, knowledge of language, and vocabulary acquisition and use. In addition, students meet writing standards as they answer questions about the passages, demonstrating their ability to convey ideas coherently, clearly, and with support from the text.

Reading Standards for Informational Text	Passages
Key Ideas and Details	
• Refer to details and examples in a text when explaining what the text says explicitly and when drawing inferences from the text.	1–20
• Determine the main idea of a text and explain how it is supported by key details; summarize the text.	1–20
• Explain events, procedures, ideas, or concepts in a historical, scientific, or technical text, including what happened and why, based on specific information in the text.	1–11, 13–20
Craft and Structure	
• Determine the meaning of general academic and domain-specific words or phrases in a text relevant to a grade 4 topic or subject area.	1–20
• Describe the overall structure (e.g., chronology, comparison, cause/effect, problem/solution) of events, ideas, concepts, or information in a text or part of a text.	1–20
Integration of Knowledge and Ideas	
• Interpret information presented visually, orally, or quantitatively (e.g., in charts, graphs, diagrams, time lines, animations, or interactive elements on Web pages) and explain how the information contributes to an understanding of the text in which it appears.	2, 4, 7–9, 11–14, 17, 19
• Explain how an author uses reasons and evidence to support particular points in a text.	1–20
Range of Reading and Level of Text Complexity	
• By the end of the year, read and comprehend informational texts, including history/social studies, science, and technical texts, in the grades 4–5 text complexity band proficiently, with scaffolding as needed at the high end of the range.	1–20

Source: © Copyright 2010 National Governors Association Center for Best Practices and Council of Chief State School Officers. All rights reserved.

Main Idea & Details

Every passage has one or more main ideas supported by details. The main idea answers the question, "Who (or What) is this piece about?"

- The **main idea** is the most important point an author makes about a topic. The main idea in most paragraphs is stated in a *topic sentence*. The topic sentence can appear anywhere in a paragraph.

- **Supporting details** are facts, statements, examples, descriptions, and other information that tell more about the main idea.

Sequence of Events

As you read, notice the order in which things happen or ideas are presented. Think about the *beginning*, *middle*, and *end*.

- **Events** are the important actions that happen.

- The **sequence** is the order in which events happen.

- **Signal words** give clues that help clarify the order of events. Examples include *first, second, third, next, then, last, later, before, prior to, soon, during, while, after, finally*, as well as specific dates and times.

Fact & Opinion

Do you truly *know* something or do you simply *believe* it? Telling the difference between knowing and believing is a critical reading and thinking skill.

- A **fact** is a statement you can prove or verify. Facts are true and certain.

- An **opinion** is a statement of personal belief or feeling. Opinions vary.

- **Signal words** can help distinguish facts from opinions.

  Examples for facts: *proof, know,* and *discovered,* as well as details, such as dates and ages.

  Examples for opinions: *believe, wish, favor, expect, agree, disagree, probably, seems to, sense, think, viewpoint,* and *feel.*

Compare & Contrast

Authors discuss people, places, objects, or ideas by describing how they are alike and ways they differ.

- To **compare** means to tell how two or more things are alike.

- To **contrast** means to tell how two or more things are different.

- **Signal words** guide you to compare and contrast.

  Examples for comparing: *both, like, alike, also, too, share, in the same way,* and *similarly.*

  Examples for contrasting: *but, only, unlike, instead, however, in contrast, different, although, on the other hand, as opposed to, neither, whereas, while,* and *rather.*

Cause & Effect

A text may discuss the relationship between something that happens and any outcomes that follow from it.

- A **cause** is an event, condition, reason, or situation that makes something happen.

- An **effect** is the result of that particular event, condition, reason, or situation.

- **Signal words** are clues that help link a cause with its effects. Examples include *due to, as a result, since, therefore, because of, so, for this reason, consequently, so that, in order to,* and *leads to.*

Context Clues

Authors may use words you don't know. Search for synonyms, antonyms, explanations, or examples in the nearby text to help you figure out the meaning.

- **Context** refers to the words and sentences around the unfamiliar word.

- **Context clues** are specific indications in the text that can help you unlock the meaning of an unfamiliar word.

Problem & Solution

This kind of writing presents a challenging situation to engage readers, then offers one or more forms of resolution.

- A **problem** is a difficulty or setback situation that needs fixing.

- A **solution** is a way to deal with the problem to make things better.

- **Signal words** are clues that indicate a problem and its solutions.

  Examples for problems: *question, challenge, dilemma, issue, puzzle, need,* and *trouble.*

  Examples for solutions: *answer, result, one reason, solve, improve, fix, remedy, respond,* and *led to.*

Summarize

Think about how to retell the key ideas of a passage in your own words. Leave out unimportant details and get to the point.

- The **topic** is the focus of the passage—what it is mainly about.

- **Important details** add more information about the topic.

- A **summary** is a brief statement of the topic using its most essential details. A good summary is short, clear, and recalls what is most important.

Make Inferences

Authors may hint at an idea without stating it directly. You must use what you already know about a topic to "read between the lines" to figure out an unstated idea.

- **Text clues** are words or details that help you figure out unstated ideas.

- You **make an inference** by combining text clues with your background knowledge to come to a logical conclusion, or "educated guess."

Author's Purpose

Every author has goals in mind before writing. Close reading and common sense can help you figure out the author's intention.

- The **author's purpose** is the reason the author chose to write a particular piece. An author may write with more than one purpose.

- The main purposes for writing are to **inform** (tell, describe), to **persuade** (convince, influence), or to **entertain** (amuse, please).

- **Text clues** are words or sentences that reveal the author's purpose.

Informational
Text Passages

Name _____ Date _____

"How Did That Taste, Doggie?"

Read the life science essay.
Then follow the directions in the Text Marking box.

If you have ever spent any time with dogs, you have noticed how much better their sense of smell is than yours. They can smell things before you do. They can detect smells that you cannot. But how does a dog's sense of taste compare with ours?

Their sense of taste is not as good as ours. You get one clue simply by watching them gobble up food as if they are starving and don't seem to even taste what they are wolfing down. Well, dogs just don't seem to care much about taste. That's because they have fewer taste buds than you do.

Taste buds are groups of cells that let us know how things taste. They tell us whether foods are sweet, salty, sour, bitter, or savory. Taste buds are located on the surface of the tongue. There are also some on the roof of the mouth and in the back of the mouth. The more taste buds you have, the better your sense of taste is. Whereas humans have about 9,000 of these, canines have about 1,700.

But compared to cats, dogs are foodies. Poor cats have only about 470 taste buds in their mouths.

A puppy wolfing down dinner

⭐ Text Marking

Find the main idea and supporting details.

⬭ Circle the main idea in each paragraph.

_____ Underline supporting details for each main idea.

"How Did That Taste, Doggie?"

▶ **Answer each question. Give evidence from the essay.**

1 Which of the following words has the same meaning as *detect* (paragraph 1)?

　○ A. avoid　　　○ B. enjoy　　　○ C. identify　　　○ D. taste

What in the text helped you answer? _____

_____

_____

2 Which statement is *true* about the connection between number of taste buds and the ability to taste different things?

　○ A. An animal with more taste buds has a weaker sense of taste.

　○ B. An animal with more taste buds senses more kinds of smells.

　○ C. The fewer taste buds an animal has, the weaker its sense of taste.

　○ D. There is no connection because all animals can taste the same things.

What in the text helped you answer? _____

_____

_____

3 In your own words, explain what you think it means to "wolf down" food.

_____

_____

_____

_____

4 Suggest a different title that would work for this piece. Explain your thinking.

_____

_____

_____

_____

Informational Passages for Text Marking & Close Reading: Grade 4
© 2015 by Scholastic Teaching Resources

Name _____ Date _____

Towers of Green

Read the architecture essay.
Then follow the directions in the Text Marking box.

Most people would describe farms as huge outdoor fields for growing crops. Farms are mostly horizontal—flat spaces on the land. A vertical farm is a new way to bring farms to cities. Most cities are crowded and lack open spaces, you say. No problem! Vertical farms are flat fields hung from a towering skyscraper.

Supporters of vertical farming envision many benefits for their futuristic idea. First, crops would grow closer to where most people live, saving money and energy now used to transport crops. Next, vertical farming would provide jobs for city workers. And vertical farms would use far less water than traditional farms do.

Architects in Seoul, South Korea, are designing what they call the Urban Skyfarm. It resembles a massive tree that supports 24 acres of "fields" for growing food. The "trunk" has rooms for indoor growing. The "canopy" holds solar panels and wind engines needed to make clean energy. The "branches" are open-air terraces, stacked one above another, where plants can grow.

The architects see other uses for vertical farms. They could provide spaces for community gardens, public parks, learning centers, and farmers' markets. Architects hope that vertical farms will become a major solution to food shortages.

Design for the Urban Skyfarm

Text Marking

Find the main idea and supporting details.

◯ Circle the main idea in each paragraph.

_____ Underline supporting details for each main idea.

Towers of Green

▶ **Answer each question. Give evidence from the essay.**

1 Which statement about vertical farms is supported by information in the text?

○ A. Vertical farms cost millions of dollars to build.

○ B. Vertical farming is nothing like horizontal farming.

○ C. Vertical farms were invented in Seoul, South Korea.

○ D. Vertical farms would provide jobs and save water and energy.

What in the text helped you answer? _____

_____

_____

2 Which part of a tree is most likely the *canopy* (paragraph 3)?

○ A. the very top ○ B. the sturdy bark ○ C. the hidden roots ○ D. the green terraces

What in the text helped you answer? _____

_____

_____

3 In your own words, explain why vertical farms make sense for big cities.

_____

_____

_____

_____

4 Make an inference using the text and the picture. Why would a vertical farm need less water than a traditional farm would?

_____

_____

_____

_____

Accidents Happen

Read the health and safety article.
Then follow the directions in the Text Marking box.

What if you scrape your shin or a pet claws you by mistake? Alas, accidents occur to everyone. Minor wounds need TLC— tender loving care—and sufficient time to mend. Luckily, you can manage most small wounds without visiting a hospital; that's why it's a good idea to have basic first-aid supplies on hand at home.

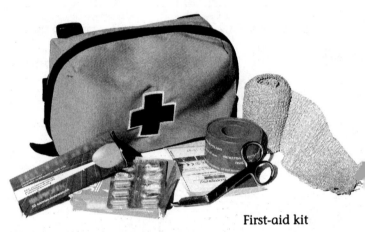

First-aid kit

The first thing to do is to stop any bleeding immediately. Small cuts and scrapes usually close on their own. If not, cover the wound with a clean cloth or bandage. Then press gently on it until the bleeding stops. This could take a few seconds or minutes.

Next, it's essential to rinse the wound to avoid infection. Use lukewarm water and mild soap to gently clean the area; repeat to remove dirt and grit. If needed, wet some cotton or gauze with alcohol or peroxide and lightly clean again. Dry the area thoroughly.

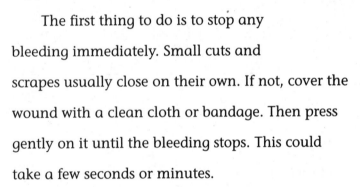

Text Marking

Find the sequence of steps.

☐ Box the signal words.

_____ Underline the important steps.

1-2-3 Number the events in the sequence they happen.

Then, cover the wound to keep out harmful germs using a bandage, gauze pad, or other type of clean cover, but don't make it too tight.

Finally, be kind to your wound. Try not to bump it. When the bandage gets wet or dirty, replace it. After a scab forms, expose the wound to fresh air so it can finish healing.

Informational Passages for Text Marking & Close Reading: Grade 4
© 2015 by Scholastic Teaching Resources

Name _____ Date _____

Accidents Happen

▶ **Answer each question. Give evidence from the article.**

1 Which of the following words means about the same as *sufficient*, as used in paragraph 1?

○ A. enough   ○ B. scarce   ○ C. painful   ○ D. restful

What in the text helped you answer? _____

_____

_____

2 Which is the *last* thing to do when caring for a wound?

○ A. Rinse the wound carefully.   ○ C. Press on the wound to stop any bleeding.

○ B. Let the wound get some fresh air.   ○ D. Apply some form of cover to the wound.

What in the text helped you answer? _____

_____

_____

_____

3 According to the article, what is the most important reason to clean and cover a wound?

_____

_____

_____

_____

4 Does the advice explained in this article apply to all kinds of accidents? In your own words, explain your response.

_____

_____

_____

_____

_____

Informational Passages for Text Marking & Close Reading: Grade 4

Bigger and Better

Read the technology article.
Then follow the directions in the Text Marking box.

Back in 1927, Americans got their first peek at television. On this electronic wonder with its 2-inch by 3-inch screen, a fortunate few watched a speech in black-and-white given by Herbert Hoover.

A decade later, people could watch on slightly larger sets, some with 9-inch screens (measured diagonally). They watched in astonishment. But television was still in its infancy. Very few families owned a set.

After World War II, TV sales skyrocketed; about 1 in 200 families nationwide had one. That number leaped to more than 9 in 10 households by the 1960s, when TV screens got much larger. Then, with the arrival of color, fascination increased again. Yet, there were very few channels people could watch.

With the coming of cable in the 1970s, the number of channels multiplied. Then, in the 1980s, TV viewing itself changed with

1949 TV set in a large *console*

Text Marking

Find the sequence of events.

☐ Box the signal words.

_____ <u>Underline</u> the important events.

1-2-3 Number the events in the sequence they happened.

the invention of devices that let people record programs and then watch them whenever they wished. Next, in the late 1990s, new high-definition television changed the game again. These HDTVs displayed clearer, sharper pictures on even larger, flat-panel screens. Today, with further improvements in technology, TVs are linked to computers and the Internet.

What's next for TV?

Informational Passages for Text Marking & Close Reading: Grade 4
© 2015 by Scholastic Teaching Resources

Bigger and Better

▶ **Answer each question. Give evidence from the article.**

1 Look at the photo and its caption. Which is the best synonym for *console*?

○ A. cabinet   ○ B. furniture   ○ C. opening   ○ D. window

What in the text helped you answer? _____

_____

_____

2 Which of the following statements is *true* about the earliest televisions?

○ A. They showed color images.   ○ C. They got their power from gasoline.

○ B. They had very small screens.   ○ D. You could find them in nearly every home.

What in the text helped you answer? _____

_____

_____

_____

3 Make an inference. What led to each new rise in interest for television? Support your idea.

_____

_____

_____

_____

_____

4 Compare and contrast early televisions with today's TVs.

_____

_____

_____

_____

_____

Name _____   Date _____

Time to Learn

Read the debate speech.
Then follow the directions in the Text Marking box.

I believe that American students need to spend more time in school. We need it to keep up with students all over the world. And the following facts support my views.

American students are in school for about 6 hours a day, 180 days a year. In Germany, the school year lasts 240 days; in Japan and South Korea, it lasts for more than 200 days. In France, the school day is 8 hours long, plus kids have a half-day every Saturday. Chinese students are in class 9 hours each day, 260 days a year.

Test scores show that we are falling behind students in many other countries. This is both sad and unnecessary. To keep up, I think we must extend our school year and lengthen each school day. We do not need all those hours we spend playing video games or watching dumb TV shows. We should be more productive by sharpening our math skills or becoming better readers. We can do it—we just need more time.

I acknowledge that other factors, like well-qualified teachers and supportive homes, are important to helping kids learn. But if we don't add more school time, we'll keep falling behind.

Text Marking

Identify the facts and opinions in the speech.

▭ Box at least three signal words or phrases.

◯ Circle at least three facts.

▁▁▁ <u>Underline</u> at least three opinions.

Informational Passages for Text Marking & Close Reading: Grade 4
© 2015 by Scholastic Teaching Resources

Time to Learn

▶ **Answer each question. Give evidence from the speech.**

1 Which of the following words means about the same as *acknowledge* (paragraph 4)?

○ A. argue   ○ B. learn   ○ C. question   ○ D. recognize

What in the text helped you answer? _____

_____

_____

2 Why does the debater argue that American test scores are lower than test scores in other countries?

○ A. Foreign students have more days of school than American students have.

○ B. Foreign students are far smarter than American students are.

○ C. American students start school later.

○ D. American tests are much too difficult.

What in the text helped you answer? _____

_____

_____

3 Summarize the debater's point of view on how American kids spend their free time.

_____

_____

_____

_____

4 In your own words, explain how you can tell a fact from an opinion in this speech.

_____

_____

_____

_____

Name _____   Date _____

Restart the Music!

Read the business letter.
Then follow the directions in the Text Marking box.

Dear Superintendent Calderón,

I am discouraged that our school's music programs have been cut. As the father of three children, I know how much my kids need music. In my view, music is not an unnecessary frill, as critics say. As I see it, music is as vital as reading, writing, and math. I believe music helps children grow socially, emotionally, and academically.

Serious brain science supports my view. Dr. Nina Kraus, researcher at Northwestern University, has long studied how learning music affects growing brains. Her findings prove that it does enhance students' brains and nervous systems. These benefits improve children's abilities in language, memory, patterning, and critical listening. She supports music training as part of a balanced school program. I strongly agree. I favor all the brain development kids can get!

My kids sang nearly as soon as they could speak. They learned new words from song lyrics. They exercised their bodies and minds dancing to DVDs and music videos. They sang songs to memorize math facts. In my opinion, these are perfect examples of music working its magic.

A 1997 study by research teams from Wisconsin and California found that music increases spatial reasoning, which links to stronger math and science skills. Is this not proof enough that our schools deserve music for all?

Respectfully yours,

James Gosch

(Father of Brianna, Luke, and Nelson)

Text Marking

Identify the facts and opinions in the speech.

☐ Box at least three signal words or phrases.

⬭ Circle at least three facts.

___ Underline at least three opinions.

Restart the Music!

▶ **Answer each question. Give evidence from the letter.**

1 Which of the following is most nearly *opposite* in meaning to *vital*, as used in paragraph 1?

○ A. energetic ○ B. musical ○ C. unhealthy ○ D. unnecessary

What in the text helped you answer? _____

_____

_____

2 Why did Mr. Gosch discuss research by Dr. Nina Kraus in paragraph 2?

○ A. He is a music lover himself. ○ C. He agrees with her research findings.

○ B. He went to Northwestern University. ○ D. He hopes his children will become musicians.

What in the text helped you answer? _____

_____

_____

_____

3 Why do you think Mr. Gosch shared his memories of his children as "perfect examples of music working its magic"?

_____

_____

_____

_____

4 Explain how the last paragraph of the letter summarizes Mr. Gosch's point of view.

_____

_____

_____

_____

_____

Informational Passages for Text Marking & Close Reading: Grade 4
© 2015 by Scholastic Teaching Resources

Which Boat?

Read the blog post.
Then follow the directions in the Text Marking box.

Rowboat

I just had a great weekend at a lake cabin where I got an introduction to boating. I now know differences between a rowboat and a canoe. But let me first describe how they are alike.

Each is small enough to be handled by one or two people. Both vessels are the right size for a small lake and require muscle power to make them go. Neither has an engine or a sail.

But the two water craft differ in important ways. First, the canoe is lightweight; it has a tapered bottom and is pointed at either end. In contrast, the heavier rowboat has a flat bottom and is pointed only in the front. Each vessel requires a special device to propel it through the water. To move a canoe, each person uses one paddle and switches it from side to side to steer. But to move a rowboat, a rower uses two oars at once, one on each side of the boat.

Canoe

Safety is another contrast between the canoe and rowboat. The rowboat is sturdier, which makes it safer. On the other hand, the lighter canoe can go faster, but is harder to steer and can more easily tip over.

I preferred the rowboat because I was better able to control it.

Text Marking

Compare and contrast rowboats and canoes.

☐ Box at least three signal words or phrases.

◯ Circle at least three ways they are alike.

___ Underline at least three ways they are different.

Name _____ Date _____

Which Boat?

▶ **Answer each question. Give evidence from the blog.**

1 Which of the following words in the piece best helps you determine the meaning of *vessel* (paragraph 2)?

○ A. boating   ○ B. device   ○ C. engine   ○ D. paddle

What in the text helped you answer? _____

_____

_____

2 Which is a similarity between canoes and rowboats?

○ A. Both have flat bottoms and two pointed ends.   ○ C. Both are powered by engines or sails.

○ B. Both move equally fast through the water.   ○ D. Both are a good size for lake use.

What in the text helped you answer? _____

_____

_____

3 In your own words, explain the different ways you make the two boats move.

_____

_____

_____

_____

4 Contrast the photos of the canoe and rowboat. What other differences do you notice?

_____

_____

_____

_____

_____

Informational Passages for Text Marking & Close Reading: Grade 4
© 2015 by Scholastic Teaching Resources

Your Move

Read the games article.
Then follow the directions in the Text Marking box.

Checkers set

Chess set

Checkers and chess have many things in common. But these two popular board games have a number of key differences, too.

Players and Board Both games are for two players who sit at opposite sides of a square board. Its same-sized small squares alternate—dark and light. In both games, players take turns moving their pieces according to the rules.

Pieces and Movements In checkers, each player begins with 12 flat, round pieces called *men*. One player has all dark pieces, the other, all light ones. To start, men are set out on alternating squares across the three rows nearest each player. All pieces move only diagonally.

Like checkers sets, chess sets come in two opposite colors. But in contrast, each chess player gets 16 pieces to arrange in two rows. Pieces are not all the same. Instead, one row holds the eight larger pieces: two rooks, two knights, two bishops,

---

★ Text Marking ★

Compare and contrast the games of checkers and chess.

☐ Box at least four signal words or phrases.

⬭ Circle at least three ways they are alike.

___ Underline at least three ways they are different.

---

one queen, and one king. The eight smaller pieces, or pawns, fill another row. Each type of piece has its own particular way to move. For instance, bishops move diagonally over one or several squares, while pawns move only one square at a time.

To Win A checkers game ends when one player captures all the other's men. However, the winner in chess is the one who captures the opponent's king.

Informational Passages for Text Marking & Close Reading: Grade 4
© 2015 by Scholastic Teaching Resources

Your Move

▶ **Answer each question. Give evidence from the article.**

1 Which of the following direction words best describes how checkers pieces move on the board?

○ A. horizontally   ○ B. vertically   ○ C. diagonally   ○ D. circularly

What in the text helped you answer? _____

_____

_____

2 In which way are chess pieces unlike checkers pieces?

○ A. Chess pieces are played on a square board.   ○ C. Chess sets cost more than checkers sets.

○ B. Chess pieces come in six different shapes.   ○ D. Chess pieces are all the same color.

What in the text helped you answer? _____

_____

_____

3 Study the photographs of the playing boards. Describe them in as many specific ways as you can.

_____

_____

_____

_____

_____

4 Look back at your text markings and think about the ideas in the article. In your own words, summarize the similarities and the major differences between chess and checkers.

_____

_____

_____

_____

When It's 10 AM in…

Read the geography essay.
Then follow the directions in the Text Marking box.

Time zones are geographical areas in which one common time is used. The world is divided into 24 time zones. There are six in the United States: Eastern, Central, Mountain, Pacific, Alaska, and Hawaii-Aleutian. When it is noon in New York City, it is 11 AM in Chicago, 10 AM in Denver, 9 AM in San Diego, 8 AM in Anchorage, and 7 AM in Honolulu.

Before there were time zones, towns and cities used their own time standards; they set their clocks to local sunrises and sunsets, though these events differed from place to place. The effect was that separate towns had their own times. For a while, it didn't matter too much because snail-like travel speeds made time differences in distant locations hardly noticeable.

But since the coming of railroads, time variations between locations began to matter. In the late 1800s, there were more than 300 regional "sun times" in the United States. These differences caused chaos for railroad timetables. Uniform schedules for departures and arrivals were sorely needed.

In 1883, American and Canadian railroad companies adopted four time zones. The time was the same anywhere within each zone. This decision resulted in less confusion. Now travelers could easily know the correct time at their destination.

Pacific Time | Mountain Time | Central Time | Eastern Time

Chicago, Denver, New York, San Diego

Hawaii-Aleutian Time — Honolulu — Anchorage — Alaska Time

Six U.S. Time Zones
[Standard times shown]

Text Marking

Find at least two cause-and-effect relationships.

☐ Box at least four signal words or phrases.

◯ Circle the causes.

___ Underline the effects.

ı It's 10 AM in...

► Answer each o⬚⬚⬚ ⬚idence from the essay.

1 Which is⬚ ⬚⬚⬚ *uniform*, as it is used in paragraph 3?

○ A. ⬚⬚⬚   ○ B. consistent   ○ C. haphazard   ○ D. published

Wh⬚ ⬚⬚⬚ ⬚lped you answer? _____

_____

2 ⬚⬚⬚ ⬚he Eastern Time Zone. Oregon is in the Pacific Time Zone. If it is 9 AM
⬚⬚⬚ ⬚and, Ohio, what time is it in Salem, Oregon?

/ AM   ○ B. 8 AM   ○ C. 6 AM   ○ D. 5 AM

⬚at in the text helped you answer? _____

_____

_____

3 Reread the opening paragraph and use the time-zone map. Explain why the author
listed the times in those particular cities in the order you see.

_____

_____

_____

_____

_____

4 What made train scheduling so difficult before time zones came into effect?

_____

_____

_____

_____

_____

Pop Culture

Read the culture article.
Then follow the directions in the Text Marking box.

Americans love popcorn; we consume more of it than people do anywhere else in the world—16 billion quarts a year! We also love going to the movies. But at first, popcorn and movie theaters did not go together.

As movie-going became a popular activity, luxurious movie theaters popped up across the country. People flocked to these glamorous places with their elaborate decorations, crystal chandeliers, and grand staircases. The last thing theater owners wanted was the challenge of crumbs on the plush velvet seats and expensive red carpets. For that reason, patrons were asked not to bring food into theaters.

But that all changed in the 1930s, when a few bold theater owners allowed popcorn stands in their movie palaces. As a result, attendance rose and profits soared. (And so did the piles of crumbs!) Popcorn and movies began a lasting relationship. By the 1940s, the smell of melted butter wafted from most theater lobbies.

Text Marking

Find at least two cause-and-effect relationships.

☐ Box at least four signal words or phrases.

◯ Circle the causes.

__ Underline the effects.

The hefty profits popcorn sales brought had three clear effects. One was that movie theater concessions began selling other foods and beverages. Another was that movie prices dropped—at least for a while. And a third effect was that movie theaters needed constant cleaning.

Informational Passages for Text Marking & Close Reading: Grade 4
© 2015 by Scholastic Teaching Resources

Name _____ Date _____

Pop Culture

▶ **Answer each question. Give evidence from the article.**

1 When their profits are *hefty* (paragraph 4), movie theater owners

◯ A. had financial troubles.　　◯ C. needed to raise ticket prices.

◯ B. removed the messy carpets.　◯ D. took in huge sums of money.

What in the text helped you answer? _____

_____

_____

2 Why did popcorn and movie theaters not go together at first?

◯ A. Owners didn't want to dirty up their grand theaters.

◯ B. Theaters had no room for popcorn stands.

◯ C. Popcorn was not a popular snack food.

◯ D. Popcorn hadn't been invented yet.

What in the text helped you answer? _____

_____

_____

3 Explain why movie theaters came to need regular cleaning.

_____

_____

_____

4 Make an inference. Why do you think that movie theater ticket prices fell after popcorn was first introduced to theater audiences?

_____

_____

_____

_____

Informational Passages for Text Marking & Close Reading: Grade 4
© 2015 by Scholastic Teaching Resources

The Five-Second Rule

Read the health essay.
Then follow the directions in the Text Marking box.

When a person drops otherwise edible food on the floor, you might hear someone yell, "Five-second rule!" This is the belief that if you retrieve food from the floor in five seconds or less, it's still safe to eat. Is this a legitimate fact you can accept as true? Or is it simply an excuse not to waste that tasty brownie? High school senior Jillian Clarke wanted to know. She conducted a controlled scientific experiment to test this notion.

Clarke got smooth and rough tiles of equal size. First, she cleaned them thoroughly. Then she contaminated them with samples of the *E. coli* bacteria. She chose cookies and gummy bears as the test foods. In turn, she dropped one of each on the tainted tiles, picked each up in five seconds or less, and tested for the presence of *E. coli* on the foods.

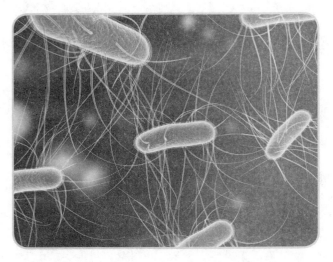

Illness-causing *E. coli* bacteria (seen through a microscope)

Text Marking

Use context clues to unlock word meanings.

◯ Circle the words *legitimate* and *contaminated*.

____ Underline context clues for each word.

The results left no doubt. Clarke found a transfer of germs in less than five seconds. Common sense prevails: It's simply not safe to eat food that has fallen on the floor. For her work, Clarke received a joke prize for "research that first makes you laugh, then makes you think."

Informational Passages for Text Marking & Close Reading: Grade 4
© 2015 by Scholastic Teaching Resources

Name _____ Date _____

The Five-Second Rule

► **Answer each question. Give evidence from the essay.**

1 Which of the following is not *edible* (paragraph 1)?

○ A. broccoli   ○ B. brownies   ○ C. floor tiles   ○ D. gummy bears

What in the text helped you answer? _____

_____

_____

2 What usually happens when people eat food that is *contaminated* with *E. coli* bacteria?

○ A. They become sick.   ○ C. They have endless hunger.

○ B. They fall on the floor.   ○ D. They perform a science experiment.

What in the text helped you answer? _____

_____

_____

3 Summarize what Jillian Clarke discovered as a result of her experiment.

_____

_____

_____

_____

_____

4 Use context clues in the essay to explain the meaning of *tainted* (paragraph 2) in your own words.

_____

_____

_____

_____

_____

Informational Passages for Text Marking & Close Reading: Grade 4

From an Egghead

Read the word origin article.
Then follow the directions in the Text Marking box.

Expressions come and go, but some are so durable that they never fade away. Because I'm a *good egg*—a friendly, reliable person—I'd like to draw attention to sayings using the word *egg*. Expressions with "egg" have been around for centuries.

Language is one of my greatest delights. I've been a fan of words ever since, as a child, I perused my dad's huge dictionary for new ones! Still, I hope I don't *lay an egg* with this topic; rather, I hope you find it amusing and interesting. Perhaps you'll add "eggy" sayings to perk up your own speaking and writing.

Yet it was like *walking on eggs* to present my idea for this article to a language magazine that has very demanding standards. The editors typically select serious pieces. So I planned my pitch, spoke carefully, and offered logical examples to make my case. I held my breath, hoping my editor wouldn't frown and order me to *go fry an egg*. Happily, her praise led to this piece.

Don't put all your eggs in one basket!

Text Marking

Use context clues to unlock the meanings of words and phrases.

◯ Circle the word *durable* and the phrases *walking on eggs* and *nest egg*.

_____ Underline context clues for each word or phrase.

I plan to tuck away the money I'll earn from this article and others to build my *nest egg*. One day, if I can save enough, I hope to buy a farm, and maybe even some hens!

Informational Passages for Text Marking & Close Reading: Grade 4
© 2015 by Scholastic Teaching Resources

Name _____ Date _____

From an Egghead

▶ **Answer each question. Give evidence from the article.**

1 According to the article, why did the author say it was like *walking on eggs* to convince a magazine's editors to accept a piece on egg expressions?

○ A. Magazine editors may not respect eggheads.

○ B. An editor's feelings can be fragile, like eggs are.

○ C. There were broken eggshells on the editor's floor.

○ D. It is worrying to present a lighthearted idea to a serious magazine because the author thought the editors might react badly.

What in the text helped you answer? _____

_____

_____

2 Which expression might the editor have used instead of *go fry an egg* (paragraph 3)?

○ A. "Get lost!"   ○ C. "Think of another topic!"

○ B. "Bring me breakfast!"   ○ D. "Tell me more egg ideas."

What in the text helped you answer? _____

_____

_____

3 Explain how you determined the meaning of *nest egg* (paragraph 4).

_____

_____

_____

_____

4 Think about the saying in the caption of the photo. In your own words, explain its meaning. Tell how the picture offers clues. Write your answer on a separate sheet of paper.

Informational Passages for Text Marking & Close Reading: Grade 4
© 2015 by Scholastic Teaching Resources

Pickles on Ice

Read the environment essay.
Then follow the directions in the Text Marking box.

Do thoroughfares in your area ice over in winter? Are sidewalks treacherous for walking? If so, would you ever think to grab a jar of pickles?

Icy roads can be dangerous. Cities and towns spend heavily each winter spreading rock salt on roads to melt the ice. However, the problem with using rock salt is that it is hazardous to the environment. Salt seeps into the ground and into our fresh water, damaging plants and trees. Salt also harms wildlife and pets.

This challenge has pushed transportation departments in some states to seek safer materials to use. One solution is to replace rock salt with *brine*. Brine is salty water. It is found in the juice of beets, pickles, potatoes, and cheese. Brine has three advantages over rock salt. First, it causes less harm to the environment. It also works better than rock salt at very low temperatures. Moreover, using brine saves money for taxpayers.

Indiana has begun to use beet brine to melt ice on its roadways. Surfaces in Tennessee are being de-iced with potato brine. New Jersey ice is being melted with pickle brine. Cheese brine is now used to combat Wisconsin's icy streets. Yes, states may have found an effective answer to a slippery problem.

Truck de-icing a road in winter

Text Marking

Find the problem and solution.

☐ Box the signal words.

◯ Circle the problem.

_____ Underline the solution.

Informational Passages for Text Marking & Close Reading: Grade 4
© 2015 by Scholastic Teaching Resources

Pickles on Ice

▶ **Answer each question. Give evidence from the essay.**

1 Which of the following is the best meaning of *brine*?

○ A. a winter danger　　　　○ C. slippery ice

○ B. liquid with salt in it　　○ D. a kind of cheese

What in the text helped you answer? _____

_____

_____

2 Why may rock salt *not* be the best way to melt ice on roads in winter?

○ A. Rock salt works too slowly.

○ B. Rock salt is the same color as ice.

○ C. Rock salt causes potholes in roads.

○ D. Rock salt can harm living things and the environment.

What in the text helped you answer? _____

_____

_____

_____

3 What transportation problems do cities and towns face in winter weather?

_____

_____

_____

4 Give three reasons from the text that explain why using brine to melt ice is a good idea.

_____

_____

_____

_____

Informational Passages for Text Marking & Close Reading: Grade 4
© 2015 by Scholastic Teaching Resources

Name _____ Date _____

Animal or Vegetable?

Read the newspaper article.
Then follow the directions in the Text Marking box.

Ivory is a natural substance known for its warm, creamy hue. For centuries, collectors traveled the world in search of it. Artisans carved and polished ivory to form unique art works and jewelry. But the problem with ivory lay in the cruel way it was obtained.

The most common source of ivory was the tusks of African elephants. Other ivory came from walrus, hippo, and rhino tusks. Sadly, the only sure way to get ivory from an animal's tusk is to kill the creature. How wrong to murder magnificent animals just to make art objects!

It took time for an acceptable solution to emerge. Interestingly, the remedy was a natural product found in the rainforests of South America. So-called vegetable ivory comes from the tagua nut. Tagua nuts grow in the fruit of a palm tree called an "elephant plant." Tagua nuts share many characteristics with ivory. Both are smooth, hard, and bone-colored. Both can be carved and polished into lovely objects.

But vegetable ivory has major advantages over animal ivory. For one thing, tagua nuts are a renewable resource. Harvesting them causes no harm to the elephant plant. Furthermore, tagua ivory is cheaper to obtain and encourages conservation of tropical rainforests.

Vegetable-ivory owl carved from tagua nut

Text Marking

Find the problem and solution.

☐ Box the signal words.

◯ Circle the problem.

___ Underline the solution.

Animal or Vegetable?

▶ **Answer each question. Give evidence from the article.**

1 Another word that means about the same as *hue* (paragraph 1) is _____.

  ○ A. finish   ○ B. taste   ○ C. color   ○ D. plant

What in the text helped you answer? _____

_____

_____

2 Which is the most important way that vegetable ivory is better than animal ivory?

  ○ A. Harvesting animal ivory damages the rainforest.

  ○ B. Vegetable ivory costs far less than animal ivory.

  ○ C. Vegetable ivory has a warmer color than animal ivory has.

  ○ D. Obtaining animal ivory causes animal cruelty while vegetable ivory is harmless.

What in the text helped you answer? _____

_____

_____

3 In what ways are animal and vegetable ivory similar?

_____

_____

_____

_____

4 Make an inference. Why do you think farmers in the rainforests of South America are eager to protect elephant plants?

_____

_____

_____

_____

Informational Passages for Text Marking & Close Reading: Grade 4
© 2015 by Scholastic Teaching Resources

Elephant Orchestra

Read the animal behavior article.
Then follow the directions in the Text Marking box.

"Elephants like music," says musician and neuroscientist David Sulzer. "If you play music, they'll come over." At a conservation center in Thailand, he saw this for himself. He watched elephant trainers sing to the animals to soothe them. Sulzer already knew that elephants could recognize melodies. He wondered if they would play music themselves.

So Sulzer collected a band of elephants at the center to find out. He first built a variety of huge, unbreakable percussion instruments the elephants could play with their trunks or feet. He built 22 such instruments. These included drums, gongs, flutes, cymbals, and king-sized xylophones the elephants could play with a large mallet. Sulzer's instruments resemble traditional Thai ones and sound like them, too.

Sulzer soon found that elephants were indeed musicians. They could bang, stomp, tap, and blow to play distinct musical notes. With the help of the trainers, Sulzer got his elephant orchestra to play Thai melodies the tuskers recognize.

The Thai Elephant Orchestra has been a success. They have made three albums. And they'll play for peanuts (or bananas or apples). But the best part is that these talented musicians help raise much-needed money to house and protect other endangered elephants.

An elephant named Pratiah playing the drums

Text Marking

Summarize the text.

◯ Circle the topic.

_____ Underline important details.

Name _____ Date _____

Elephant Orchestra

▶ **Answer each question. Give evidence from the article.**

1 The purpose of a *conservation center* (paragraph 1) is to _____.

- ○ A. soothe and calm wild animals
- ○ B. offer a safe home for wildlife
- ○ C. provide musical entertainment
- ○ D. raise funding for special equipment

What in the text helped you answer? _____

_____

_____

2 Which of the following would make another good title for this article?

- ○ A. How to Fund Conservation Centers
- ○ B. David Sulzer's Work
- ○ C. Massive Musicians
- ○ D. A Visit to Thailand

What in the text helped you answer? _____

_____

_____

3 Look back at your text markings. Write a one-paragraph summary of the key information provided in the article.

_____

_____

_____

_____

_____

4 In this article, "play for peanuts" has two meanings. Explain what they are.

_____

_____

_____

_____

Informational Passages for Text Marking & Close Reading: Grade 4
© 2015 by Scholastic Teaching Resources

Name _____ Date _____

The Man Behind Yoda

Read the biographical sketch.
Then follow the directions in the Text Marking box.

Make-up artists play an important role in movie-making. Every year, the best of them, like the best actors, directors, and screenwriters, are honored by Hollywood for their contributions. Stuart Freeborn, called by some the "grandfather of modern make-up design," may have been the best of the best.

English-born Freeborn was already famous for his imaginative work when he was hired to create characters for *Star Wars*. He'd already worked on many films and had done the make-up for scores of famous actors. This gifted artist understood faces. He knew just how to emphasize a cheekbone or arch an eyebrow.

But Stuart Freeborn is best known today for the unforgettable characters he created for the *Star Wars* movies. Fanciful creatures like Jabba the Hutt and Chewbacca were his creations. So was the tiny Jedi master, Yoda.

Stuart Freeborn with Yoda

Text Marking

Summarize the text.

◯ Circle the topic.

_____ Underline important details.

Yoda is odd-looking, with a pointed chin and wrinkles crossing his forehead. The resemblance between that charming pint-sized Jedi and Freeborn is unmistakable. That's because when coming up with a model for this now-famous face, Freeborn chose one he'd never used before—his own!

Stuart Freeborn worked on glamorous stars, superheroes, cavemen, and Muppets, too. He died in 2013, but his memorable characters will live on.

Name _____ Date _____

The Man Behind Yoda

▶ **Answer each question. Give evidence from the biographical sketch.**

1 Someone or something that is *pint-sized* (paragraph 4) is _____.

○ A. the size of a milk carton   ○ B. a fictional character   ○ C. very old   ○ D. little

What in the text helped you answer? _____

_____

2 Which of the following do Jabba the Hutt, Chewbacca, and Yoda have in common?

○ A. All three were honored in Hollywood.   ○ C. All three are real people.

○ B. All three had the same creator.   ○ D. All three are Muppets.

What in the text helped you answer? _____

_____

3 Look back at your text markings. Write a one-paragraph summary of the key information provided in the biographical sketch.

_____

_____

_____

_____

_____

4 What do people mean by calling Stuart Freeborn the "grandfather of modern make-up design"?

_____

_____

_____

_____

_____

_____

Informational Passages for Text Marking & Close Reading: Grade 4
© 2015 by Scholastic Teaching Resources

Name _____ Date _____

The Whole Bird

Read the memoir.
Then follow the directions in the Text Marking box.

No one knows who first said, "Waste not, want not," but my grandmother lived by that saying. She applied the strategy to most everything she did, especially to her cooking. Oh, what she did with chicken!

Chicken was a staple in her home, a food she served all the time. Or so it seemed to me. For dinners, she often prepared the most delicious roast chicken anyone ever ate. But that was only part of what she did with that chicken. She would use just about every part of that bird before she was done with it.

She wasted nothing, not even the extra fat, which she melted down to use in future cooking. She took out the liver and the gizzard—the bird's stomach—to save for her delicious stuffing or to flavor a meatloaf. She used the picked-over chicken carcass to make stock for soup. And, as I recall, she'd also include the bird's neck, feet, back, and wing tips for that purpose. Naturally, she used any leftover chicken meat for sandwiches, stews, or casseroles.

I try to be a smart shopper and economical cook. I don't let food go to waste. But as conscientious and frugal as I aim to be, I'll never match Grandma.

Parts of a chicken

Text Marking

Make an inference: Why does the writer admire Grandma?

_____ Underline text clues.

 Think about what you already know.

Name _____ Date _____

The Whole Bird

▶ **Answer each question. Give evidence from the memoir.**

1 Any food served regularly in a household can be called a _____.

○ A. hamburger   ○ B. leftover   ○ C. chicken   ○ D. staple

What in the text helped you answer? _____

_____

_____

2 According to the memoir, which word would best describe the writer's grandmother?

○ A. cheap   ○ B. elderly   ○ C. thrifty   ○ D. natural

What in the text helped you answer? _____

_____

_____

_____

3 Look back at your text markings and consider your own knowledge. What does the writer admire about Grandma?

_____

_____

_____

_____

4 Based on this memoir and your own knowledge, in what other ways might Grandma have applied the "waste not, want not" saying?

_____

_____

_____

_____

_____

Informational Passages for Text Marking & Close Reading: Grade 4
© 2015 by Scholastic Teaching Resources

Name _____   Date _____

Orlando Bloomed!

Read the magazine article.
Then follow the directions in the Text Marking box.

Actor Orlando Bloom

Orlando Bloom is a famous actor you may know from his roles in *The Pirates of the Caribbean* or *Lord of the Rings* films. But his life was not always so successful.

As a boy, Bloom was diagnosed with *dyslexia*, which made his school years challenging. He often felt stupid or worthless, despite his mother's steady love and support. Still, young Orlando felt anger and frustration, though he never let on to his classmates how difficult school was for him. Though he took extra classes and studied hard, his mind moved faster than his words could express. He recalls that he "had to work three times as hard to get two-thirds of the way."

He hid his problem whenever possible; he avoided reading aloud. Then Bloom discovered acting. Playing characters on stage helped him focus. Some of his fears vanished as he experienced success and respect. Through acting, Bloom was able to work around his disability, letting his creative side shine.

Bloom encourages dyslexic kids never to think they're failures, but rather to use their hurdle to find other ways to succeed. "If you can overcome this obstacle, you are going to be that much further along than anyone else," Bloom advises.

> **dyslexia:** a learning disorder that makes reading and interpreting words very difficult

 Text Marking

Make an inference: How did acting help Orlando Bloom cope with his disability?

_____ Underline text clues.

 Think about what you already know.

Name _____ Date _____

Orlando Bloomed!

▶ **Answer each question. Give evidence from the article.**

1 Which of the following is true about having a *learning disorder* (sidebar)?

○ A. It makes a person take up acting.

○ B. It makes it harder to keep up in school.

○ C. People with learning disorders cannot find work.

○ D. People with learning disorders can never learn to read.

What in the text helped you answer? _____

_____

_____

2 Which of these words can replace the word *hurdle* as it is used in paragraph 4 without changing the meaning of the sentence?

○ A. failure   ○ B. injury   ○ C. obstacle   ○ D. success

What in the text helped you answer? _____

_____

_____

3 Why do you think Orlando Bloom avoided reading aloud in class?

_____

_____

_____

_____

4 Look back at your text markings and consider your own knowledge. How did acting help Orlando Bloom cope with his disability? Explain in your own words.

_____

_____

_____

_____

Informational Passages for Text Marking & Close Reading: Grade 4
© 2015 by Scholastic Teaching Resources

Name _____ Date _____

Bugs on the Menu

Read the nutrition article.
Then follow the directions in the Text Marking box.

Here's a question for you: What food has a mild, nutty flavor, is low in fat, and is loaded with nutrients? If you answered "a cricket," you would be right on target.

"Really?" you might ask. "Yuck!" you might add.

Eating insects may seem, well, disgusting to you. But that's because you haven't been introduced to what 2 billion people around the world already know: Insects are very healthy and tasty. And they are environmentally friendly, too. Eva Muller at the United Nations agrees because she knows that insects are not only harmless to eat, but nutritious and full of protein. She adds that they are a delicacy— a special food treat—in many countries.

One reason that bugs are so high in nutrients is that you eat the entire insect, including its exoskeleton, or outer body covering. (You don't eat a whole cow, however.)

Bugs are beginning to be served in restaurants here in America. Cricket taco with guacamole and fresh cream, anyone, with some delicious "crittle"* for dessert? Come, now. Just close your eyes and take a nibble. You might be pleasantly surprised.

Fried grasshoppers, a delicacy in Brazil, Ghana, Mexico, and Thailand

> **nutrient:** a substance living things require to live and grow

Text Marking

Check to identify the author's three purposes.

- ☐ to entertain (E)
- ☐ to inform (I)
- ☐ to persuade (P)

_____ Underline text clues for each purpose. Write E, I, or P in the margin beside each clue.

---

* "Crittle" is peanut brittle flavored with chunks of cricket meat.

Name _____ Date _____

Bugs on the Menu

▶ **Answer each question. Give evidence from the article.**

1 When would you be most likely to enjoy a *delicacy* (paragraph 3)?

○ A. on a desert hike   ○ C. while at a highway rest stop

○ B. during a holiday party   ○ D. during lunch in a school cafeteria

What in the text helped you answer? _____

_____

_____

2 According to the article, which is *not* a reason to eat insects?

○ A. Eating insects is environmentally friendly.   ○ C. Insects can be very tasty.

○ B. Insects are very cheap to buy.   ○ D. Insects are very healthy.

What in the text helped you answer? _____

_____

_____

3 Look back at how the author began the article. How would you describe the purpose of starting that way?

_____

_____

_____

_____

4 Look back at your text markings regarding author's purpose. Summarize the author's point of view about eating insects.

_____

_____

_____

_____

_____

Name _____ Date _____

A Star of the Future?

Read the sports essay.
Then follow the directions in the Text Marking box.

The 2014 Little League World Series caught the attention of a whole nation, thanks to Mo'ne Davis, a bundle of talent throwing pitches 70 miles per hour. Displaying skills equal to those of any boy in the tournament, Mo'ne became an overnight sensation. Her impressive feats landed her on the cover of *Sports Illustrated* magazine.

Mo'ne on the mound

But will her awesome talent lead to further successes in baseball? Will she go on to become the first woman ever to pitch in the Major Leagues?

Some think she might. But expecting Mo'ne to reach the Majors is unrealistic. The reason has to do with biology. At 13, girls are likely to be as tall and as strong as boys their age. The more opportunities young women get to play against boys, the more they will show that they are equal to the task. But this all seems to change with age.

As boys and girls age, clear differences in size and strength emerge. The best male ballplayers will be able to throw a ball harder and hit it farther than the best females can. So, as gifted and determined as she is, Mo'ne will not likely be able to compete successfully against Major League players.

Or will she? Only time will tell.

Text Marking

Check to identify the author's two purposes.

☐ to entertain (E)

☐ to inform (I)

☐ to persuade (P)

_____ Underline text clues for each purpose. Write E, I, or P in the margin beside each clue.

Informational Passages for Text Marking & Close Reading: Grade 4
© 2015 by Scholastic Teaching Resources

Name _____ Date _____

A Star of the Future?

▶ **Answer each question. Give evidence from the essay.**

1 Which is another word that means the same as *feats*, as it is used in paragraph 1?

○ A. accomplishments   ○ B. adventures   ○ C. pitches   ○ D. opportunities

What in the text helped you answer? _____

_____

_____

2 What does the author think will happen if more 13-year-old girls compete in sports against boys their own age?

○ A. Girls will give up because they can't keep up with the boys.

○ B. There will be fewer men wanting to coach Little League teams.

○ C. More girls will prove that they can compete successfully against boys.

○ D. More girls will become better athletes than boys their age.

What in the text helped you answer? _____

_____

_____

3 Look back at your text markings regarding author's purpose. Summarize the author's reasons why Mo'ne is not likely to become a Major League pitcher.

_____

_____

_____

_____

4 Notice how the essay ends. What do you think this says about the author's point of view on Mo'ne Davis's chances in the future?

_____

_____

_____

Answer Key

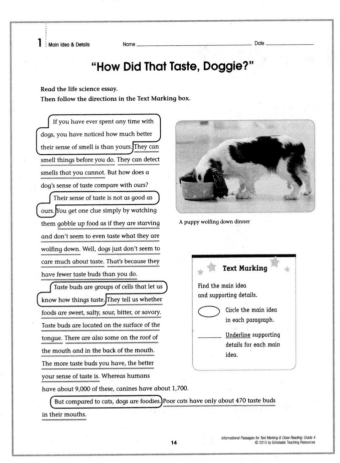

Sample Text Markings

Passage 1: "How Did That Taste, Doggie?"

1. C; Sample answer: This paragraph talks about how much better dogs can smell than we can. I used context clues in the text to figure out that C is the correct answer. Also, *detect* reminds me of *detective*, and detectives try to identify clues.

2. C; Sample answer: In paragraph 3, the author writes, "the more taste buds you have, the better your sense of taste is."

3. Sample answer: I think it means to gobble the food down as fast as possible. It probably comes from wolves in the wild eating very quickly before others try to take their food.

4. Accept reasonable responses. Sample answer: I might call the essay "All About Taste Buds" because it is mostly about how the number of taste buds affects how well an animal can taste different flavors.

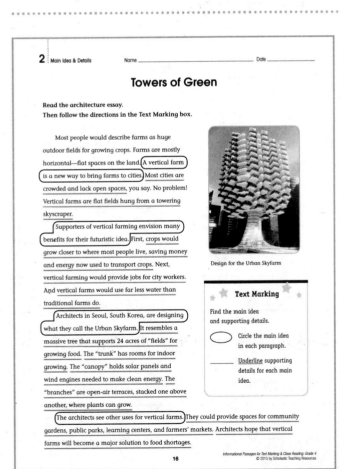

◀ Sample Text Markings

Passage 2: Towers of Green

1. D; Sample answer: It says in paragraph 2 that vertical farms could provide jobs and use less water.

2. A; Sample answer: The text compares the Skyfarm to a tree and mentions parts, like the trunk, branches, and canopy, so the canopy is probably the top. Plus, since the canopy holds solar panels, it makes sense that this is at the top where it can catch sunlight.

3. Sample answer: I think they make sense in crowded cities that don't have a lot of open space for traditional farms. Vertical farms would be more likely to fit.

4. Sample answer: It seems like the vertical farm would grow more crops in a smaller space so there is less wasted water. Also, it looks like water could probably drip down to layers below.

Passage 3: Accidents Happen

1. A; Sample answer: It takes time for a wound to heal so the other choices don't make sense. The word *enough* was the best choice to mean the same as *sufficient*.

2. B; Sample answer: Each of the other choices describes something to do earlier in the process of caring for a wound.

3. Sample answer: You need to clean the wound to help avoid infection and cover it to keep germs from getting into the wound before it is healed.

4. Sample answer: I think that the advice in this article is only for minor wounds. The author repeats the words *minor* and *small*. And I know that some injuries—like a broken leg or bad burn—need a doctor or a hospital visit.

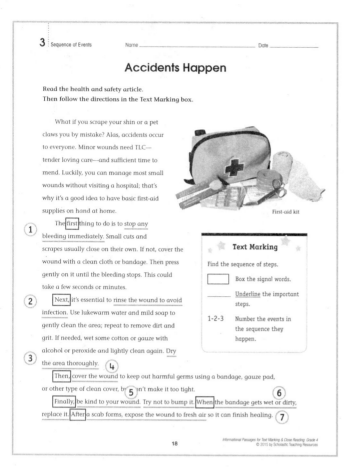

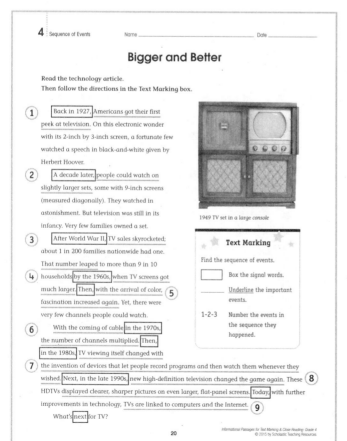

Passage 4: Bigger and Better

1. A; Sample answer: *Cabinet* fits best to replace *console* in the caption. The TV in the photo is in the console.

2. B; Sample answer: It says in paragraphs 1 and 2 that early TVs were very small; the other choices were not true about them.

3. Sample answer: I think that every time there was something new about or on television, people got excited and wanted to be part of it. For example, people got excited when color TVs were introduced.

4. Sample answer: All televisions show a moving picture with sound. But the early sets had very small screens that only showed pictures in black-and-white. Also, they could not record, did not have high definition, and had few channels to watch. TVs today have all of those things *and* can link to the Internet. Some are gigantic, too.

Informational Passages for Text Marking & Close Reading: Grade 4
© 2015 by Scholastic Teaching Resources

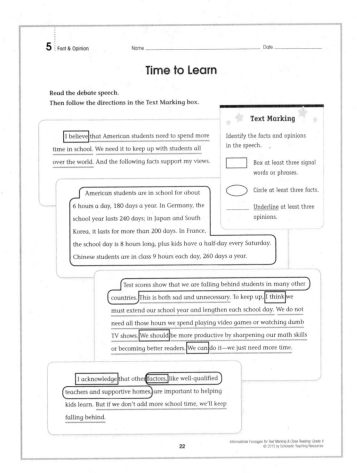

5 Fact & Opinion Name _____ Date _____

Time to Learn

Read the debate speech.
Then follow the directions in the Text Marking box.

I believe that American students need to spend more time in school. We need it to keep up with students all over the world. And the following facts support my views.

American students are in school for about 6 hours a day, 180 days a year. In Germany, the school year lasts 240 days; in Japan and South Korea, it lasts for more than 200 days. In France, the school day is 8 hours long, plus kids have a half-day every Saturday. Chinese students are in class 9 hours each day, 260 days a year.

Test scores show that we are falling behind students in many other countries. This is both sad and unnecessary. To keep up, I think we must extend our school year and lengthen each school day. We do not need all those hours we spend playing video games or watching dumb TV shows. We should be more productive by sharpening our math skills or becoming better readers. We can do it—we just need more time.

I acknowledge that other factors, like well-qualified teachers and supportive homes, are important to helping kids learn. But if we don't add more school time, we'll keep falling behind.

Text Marking

Identify the facts and opinions in the speech.

☐ Box at least three signal words or phrases.

◯ Circle at least three facts.

<u>Underline</u> at least three opinions.

22

Informational Passages for Text Marking & Close Reading: Grade 4
© 2015 by Scholastic Teaching Resources

Passage 5. Time to Learn

1. D; Sample answer: The details in this paragraph show that the speaker recognizes other factors that are important to helping kids learn.

2. A; Sample answer: In paragraph 2, the speaker describes the greater number of days students in other countries go to school. It's one of the points the debater uses to support this view.

3. Sample answer: The speaker believes that American kids waste a lot of time when they aren't in school— like playing video games or watching dumb TV.

4. Sample answer: The speaker uses specific facts about the number of hours and days students attend schools in other countries. When giving an opinion, the debater uses judgment words that show a personal view, like *dumb, sad, I think*, and *I believe*.

6 Fact & Opinion Name _____ Date _____

Restart the Music!

Read the business letter.
Then follow the directions in the Text Marking box.

Dear Superintendent Calderón,

I am discouraged that our school's music programs have been cut. As the father of three children, I know how much my kids need music. In my view, music is not an unnecessary frill, as critics say. As I see it, music is as vital as reading, writing, and math. I believe music helps children grow socially, emotionally, and academically. Serious brain science supports my view. Dr. Nina Kraus, researcher at Northwestern University, has long studied how learning music affects growing brains. Her findings prove that it does enhance students' brains and nervous systems. These benefits improve children's abilities in language, memory, patterning, and critical listening. She supports music training as part of a balanced school program. I strongly agree. I favor all the brain development kids can get!

My kids sang nearly as soon as they could speak. They learned new words from song lyrics. They exercised their bodies and minds dancing to DVDs and music videos. They sang songs to memorize math facts. In my opinion, these are perfect examples of music working its magic.

A 1997 study by research teams from Wisconsin and California found that music increases spatial reasoning, which links to stronger math and science skills. Is this not proof enough that our schools deserve music for all?

Respectfully yours,

James Gosch

(Father of Brianna, Luke, and Nelson)

Text Marking

Identify the facts and opinions in the speech.

☐ Box at least three signal words or phrases.

◯ Circle at least three facts.

<u>Underline</u> at least three opinions.

24

Informational Passages for Text Marking & Close Reading: Grade 4
© 2015 by Scholastic Teaching Resources

Passage 6: Restart the Music!

1. D; Sample answer: *Vital* means very important, like reading, writing, and math; *unnecessary* means not needed.

2. C; Sample answer: The conclusions Dr. Kraus found in her research are facts Gosch uses to support his argument that music is important.

3. Sample answer: I think Mr. Gosch offers this information to show how his own kids benefited from using music to help them learn and grow.

4. Sample answer: The last paragraph begins with a fact Mr. Gosch finds important to his argument. It lets him end with his opinion that schools should bring back music programs.

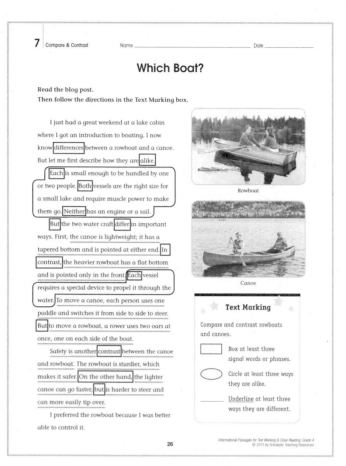

Which Boat?

Read the blog post.
Then follow the directions in the Text Marking box.

I just had a great weekend at a lake cabin where I got an introduction to boating. I now know differences between a rowboat and a canoe. But let me first describe how they are alike.

Each is small enough to be handled by one or two people. Both vessels are the right size for a small lake and require muscle power to make them go. Neither has an engine or a sail.

But the two water craft differ in important ways. First, the canoe is lightweight; it has a tapered bottom and is pointed at either end. In contrast, the heavier rowboat has a flat bottom and is pointed only in the front. Each vessel requires a special device to propel it through the water. To move a canoe, each person uses one paddle and switches it from side to side to steer. But to move a rowboat, a rower uses two oars at once, one on each side of the boat.

Safety is another contrast between the canoe and rowboat. The rowboat is sturdier, which makes it safer. On the other hand, the lighter canoe can go faster, but is harder to steer and can more easily tip over.

I preferred the rowboat because I was better able to control it.

Rowboat

Canoe

★ Text Marking

Compare and contrast rowboats and canoes.

▢ Box at least three signal words or phrases.

⬭ Circle at least three ways they are alike.

___ Underline at least three ways they are different.

Passage 7: Which Boat?

1. A; Sample answer: The word *boating* is used in paragraph 1, so I think *vessel* is a synonym for *boat*.

2. D; Sample answer: The blog says this in paragraph 2. The other choices are not similarities.

3. Sample answer: To move the rowboat, you use two oars to push against the water, one on each side of the boat. But to move a canoe, you use one or two paddles to push against the water.

4. Sample answer: It looks like the people in the canoe are facing the direction they are paddling, but the person in the rowboat is not facing the pointed part in the front of the boat. He can't see where he is going.

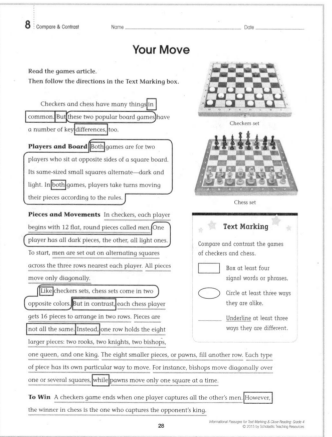

Your Move

Read the games article.
Then follow the directions in the Text Marking box.

Checkers and chess have many things in common. But these two popular board games have a number of key differences, too.

Players and Board Both games are for two players who sit at opposite sides of a square board. Its same-sized small squares alternate—dark and light. In both games, players take turns moving their pieces according to the rules.

Pieces and Movements In checkers, each player begins with 12 flat, round pieces called men. One player has all dark pieces, the other, all light ones. To start, men are set out on alternating squares across the three rows nearest each player. All pieces move only diagonally.

Like checkers sets, chess sets come in two opposite colors. But in contrast, each chess player gets 16 pieces to arrange in two rows. Pieces are not all the same. Instead, one row holds the eight larger pieces: two rooks, two knights, two bishops, one queen, and one king. The eight smaller pieces, or pawns, fill another row. Each type of piece has its own particular way to move. For instance, bishops move diagonally over one or several squares, while pawns move only one square at a time.

To Win A checkers game ends when one player captures all the other's men. However, the winner in chess is the one who captures the opponent's king.

Checkers set

Chess set

★ Text Marking

Compare and contrast the games of checkers and chess.

▢ Box at least four signal words or phrases.

⬭ Circle at least three ways they are alike.

___ Underline at least three ways they are different.

Passage 8: Your Move

1. C; Sample answer: In paragraph 3, the author says that all checkers pieces move diagonally.

2. B; Sample answer: In paragraph 4, the author mentions six different types of chess pieces, whereas all checkers men are the same size and shape.

3. Sample answers: Both boards are square and divided into 64 smaller squares. Every other small square is light or dark. Both boards have a border with letters and numbers. Each side of the checkers board has 12 playing pieces on the dark squares of the first three rows. The pieces on one side are light; those on the opposite side are dark. Each side of the chess board has 16 pieces in different shapes and sizes with light pieces on one side and dark pieces on the other. On each side, the 8 larger pieces are on the squares in the first row; the 8 smaller ones are on the squares in the second row.

4. Sample answer: Both chess and checkers are games played by two people who move pieces around on an 8 x 8 square board. But chess has more pieces with different shapes and a variety of ways to move, while checkers men are all the same size and shape and only move diagonally. Checkers and chess have different ways to get a winner.

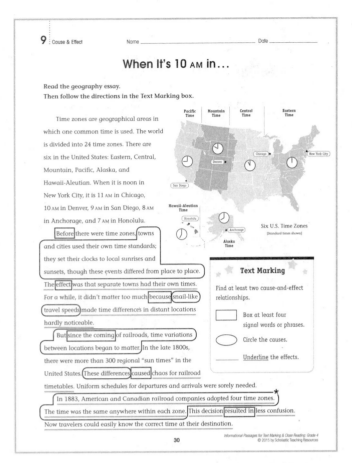

Passage 9: When It's 10 AM in…

1. B; Sample answer: The paragraph was about how hard it was for the trains dealing with all different times, so *consistent* made sense.

2. C; According to the map, places in the Pacific Time Zone are three hours earlier than the Eastern Time Zone. So 6 AM is correct.

3. Sample answer: I see from the map that each city listed is in a different time zone, and they are listed from east to west. They are also all big cities.

4. Sample answer: Before time zones, there were too many different times to make sense of. Trains couldn't set schedules, and there was a lot of confusion.

* The phrases in the passage that are circled and underlined are both causes and effects.

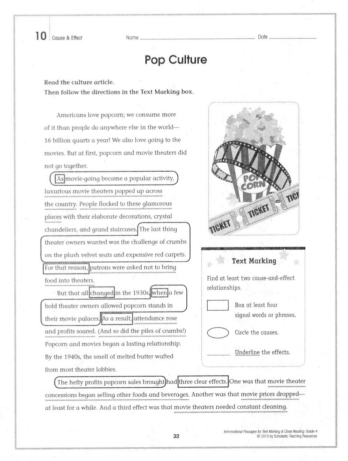

Passage 10: Pop Culture

1. D; Sample answer: I understood from context that *hefty* means large or great, so large profits means making a lot of money.

2. A; Sample answer: In paragraph 2, the author describes the fancy movie theaters that the owners wanted to keep clean.

3. Sample answer: Once people could buy and eat popcorn at the movies, and later other foods and beverages, they probably spilled and dropped stuff on the floor, seats, and carpets.

4. Sample answer: I think that since popcorn sales brought in so much more money and customers, the owners could lower ticket prices to encourage even more customers.

Sample Text Markings

Passage 11: The Five-Second Rule

1. C; Sample answer: The paragraph describes edible food versus food that is contaminated and not safe to eat. So *edible* has to do with food. Floor tiles are not food.

2. A; Sample answer: The caption of the picture explains that eating *E. coli* can make you sick.

3. Sample answer: She found that germs do attach to foods in less than five seconds, which means that the five-second rule isn't reliable.

4. Sample answer: I think *tainted* means infected with something or made unsafe. It's a synonym for *contaminated*. Clarke contaminated the tiles with *E. coli*, which tainted them.

The left portion reproduces the student worksheet pages:

11 · Context Clues

Name _____ Date _____

The Five-Second Rule

Read the health essay.
Then follow the directions in the Text Marking box.

When a person drops otherwise edible food on the floor, you might hear someone yell, "Five-second rule!" This is the belief that if you retrieve food from the floor in five seconds or less, it's still safe to eat. Is this a (legitimate) fact you can accept as true? Or is it simply an excuse not to waste that tasty brownie? High school senior Jillian Clarke wanted to know. She conducted a controlled scientific experiment to test this notion.

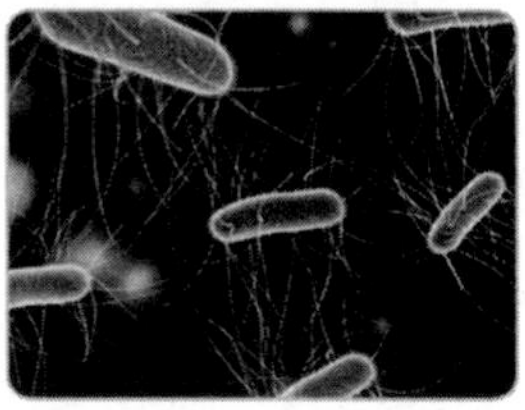

Clarke got smooth and rough tiles of equal size. First, she cleaned them thoroughly. Then she (contaminated) them with samples of the *E. coli* bacteria. She chose cookies and gummy bears as the test foods. In turn, she dropped one of each on the tainted tiles, picked each up in five seconds or less, and tested for the presence of *E. coli* on the foods.

The results left no doubt. Clarke found a transfer of germs in less than five seconds. Common sense prevails: It's simply not safe to eat food that has fallen on the floor. For her work, Clarke received a joke prize for "research that first makes you laugh, then makes you think."

Illness-causing *E. coli* bacteria (seen through a microscope)

> ★ **Text Marking** ★
>
> Use context clues to unlock word meanings.
>
> ⬭ Circle the words *legitimate* and *contaminated*.
>
> ___ Underline context clues for each word.

Informational Passages for Text Marking & Close Reading: Grade 4
© 2015 by Scholastic Teaching Resources

Sample Text Markings

Passage 12: From an Egghead

1. D; Sample answer: In paragraph 3, the author says the magazine is strict and demanding and usually picks serious pieces. The author wasn't confident the idea would be accepted.

2. A; Sample answer: I think the expression means "go away" or "stop bothering me." A is the only choice that makes sense in the context of the paragraph.

3. Sample answer: I think a *nest egg* is like a piggy bank or money-saving plan you can add to so it will grow over time. I used the text clue "if I can save enough…."

4. Sample answer: I think the saying means that you shouldn't put all your hopes, plans, or energy into just one thing, because if it goes wrong, you could lose everything. It's like if you drop the basket of eggs, most of them will probably break.

---

12 · Context Clues

Name _____ Date _____

From an Egghead

Read the word origin article.
Then follow the directions in the Text Marking box.

Expressions come and go, but some are so (durable) that they never fade away. Because I'm a *good egg*—a friendly, reliable person—I'd like to draw attention to sayings using the word *egg*. Expressions with "egg" have been around for centuries.

Language is one of my greatest delights. I've been a fan of words ever since, as a child, I perused my dad's huge dictionary for new ones! Still, I hope I don't *lay an egg* with this topic; rather, I hope you find it amusing and interesting. Perhaps you'll add "eggy" sayings to perk up your own speaking and writing.

Yet it was like (walking on eggs) to present my idea for this article to a language magazine that has very demanding standards. The editors typically select serious pieces. So I planned my pitch, spoke carefully, and offered logical examples to make my case. I held my breath, hoping my editor wouldn't frown and order me to *go fry an egg*. Happily, her praise led to this piece.

I plan to tuck away the money I'll earn from this article and others to build my (nest egg). One day, if I can save enough, I hope to buy a farm, and maybe even some hens!

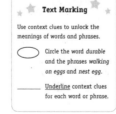

Don't put all your eggs in one basket!

> ★ **Text Marking** ★
>
> Use context clues to unlock the meanings of words and phrases.
>
> ⬭ Circle the word *durable* and the phrases *walking on eggs* and *nest egg*.
>
> ___ Underline context clues for each word or phrase.

Informational Passages for Text Marking & Close Reading: Grade 4
© 2015 by Scholastic Teaching Resources

Informational Passages for Text Marking & Close Reading: Grade 4
© 2015 by Scholastic Teaching Resources

Worksheet 13: Pickles on Ice

Pickles on Ice

Read the environment essay.
Then follow the directions in the Text Marking box.

Do thoroughfares in your area ice over in winter? Are sidewalks treacherous for walking? If so, would you ever think to grab a jar of pickles? Icy roads can be dangerous. Cities and towns spend heavily each winter spreading rock salt on roads to melt the ice. However, the problem with using rock salt is that it is hazardous to the environment. Salt seeps into the ground and into our fresh water, damaging plants and trees. Salt also harms wildlife and pets.

This challenge has pushed transportation departments in some states to seek safer materials to use. One solution is to replace rock salt with *brine*. Brine is salty water. It is found in the juice of beets, pickles, potatoes, and cheese. Brine has three advantages over rock salt. First, it causes less harm to the environment. It also works better than rock salt at very low temperatures. Moreover, using brine saves money for taxpayers.

Indiana has begun to use beet brine to melt ice on its roadways. Surfaces in Tennessee are being de-iced with potato brine. New Jersey ice is being melted with pickle brine. Cheese brine is now used to combat Wisconsin's icy streets. Yes, states may have found an effective answer to a slippery problem.

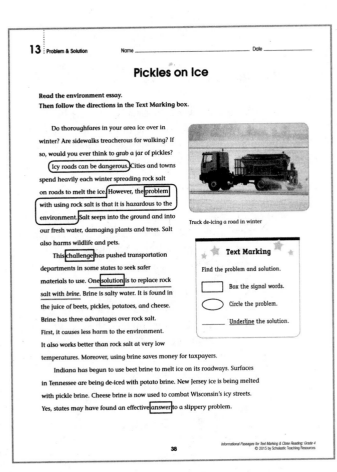

Truck de-icing a road in winter

Text Marking

Find the problem and solution.

☐ Box the signal words.

◯ Circle the problem.

___ Underline the solution.

Passage 13: Pickles on Ice

1. B; Sample answer: I saw the word *brine* in the middle of paragraph 3 and a definition of it: brine is salty water.

2. D; Sample answer: In paragraph 2, I read that salt can harm pets, plants, wildlife, and our water.

3. Sample answer: Roads and sidewalks get icy, which makes travel dangerous. But using rock salt to melt the ice harms the environment.

4. Sample answer: The article says that brine is safer for the environment, that it works better than rock salt at low temperatures, and is less expensive than rock salt.

Animal or Vegetable?

Read the newspaper article.
Then follow the directions in the Text Marking box.

Ivory is a natural substance known for its warm, creamy hue. For centuries, collectors traveled the world in search of it. Artisans carved and polished ivory to form unique art works and jewelry. But the problem with ivory lay in the cruel way it was obtained.

The most common source of ivory was the tusks of African elephants. Other ivory came from walrus, hippo, and rhino tusks. Sadly, the only sure way to get ivory from an animal's tusk is to kill the creature. How wrong to murder magnificent animals just to make art objects!

It took time for an acceptable solution to emerge. Interestingly, the remedy was a natural product found in the rainforests of South America. So-called vegetable ivory comes from the tagua nut. Tagua nuts grow in the fruit of a palm tree called an "elephant plant." Tagua nuts share many characteristics with ivory. Both are smooth, hard, and bone-colored. Both can be carved and polished into lovely objects.

But vegetable ivory has major advantages over animal ivory. For one thing, tagua nuts are a renewable resource. Harvesting them causes no harm to the elephant plant. Furthermore, tagua ivory is cheaper to obtain and encourages conservation of tropical rainforests.

Vegetable-ivory owl carved from tagua nut

Text Marking

Find the problem and solution.

☐ Box the signal words.

◯ Circle the problem.

___ Underline the solution.

Passage 14: Animal or Vegetable?

1. C; Sample answer: The context helped me know that *hue* is another word for color.

2. D; Sample answer: In paragraph 2, the article describes the cruelty involved in obtaining ivory from elephant tusks, but in paragraph 4, it states that getting tagua nuts doesn't harm the elephant plant they grow on.

3. Sample answer: Both kinds of ivory are smooth, hard, and bone-colored. Both can be carved and polished to form lovely objects.

4. Sample answer: I think that farmers can harvest and sell tagua nuts without hurting the trees, so they have a valuable crop they can use to support themselves and their families.

Sample Text Markings

15 | Summarize

Name _____ Date _____

Elephant Orchestra

Read the animal behavior article.
Then follow the directions in the Text Marking box.

"Elephants like music," says musician and neuroscientist David Sulzer. "If you play music, they'll come over." At a conservation center in Thailand, he saw this for himself. He watched elephant trainers sing to the animals to soothe them. Sulzer already knew that elephants could recognize melodies. He wondered if they would play music themselves.

So Sulzer collected a band of elephants at the center to find out. He first built a variety of huge, unbreakable percussion instruments the elephants could play with their trunks or feet. He built 22 such instruments. These included drums, gongs, flutes, cymbals, and king-sized xylophones the elephants could play with a large mallet. Sulzer's instruments resemble traditional Thai ones and sound like them, too.

Sulzer soon found that elephants were indeed musicians. They could bang, stomp, tap, and blow to play distinct musical notes. With the help of the trainers, Sulzer got his elephant orchestra to play Thai melodies the tuskers recognize.

The Thai Elephant Orchestra has been a success. They have made three albums. And they'll play for peanuts (or bananas or apples). But the best part is that these talented musicians help raise much-needed money to house and protect other endangered elephants.

An elephant named Pratiah playing the drums

★ **Text Marking** ★

Summarize the text.

◯ Circle the topic.

___ Underline important details.

◀ Sample Text Markings

Passage 15: Elephant Orchestra

1. B; Sample answer: At the end of the article, the author talks about raising money "to house and protect endangered elephants."

2. C; Sample answer: It's the only choice that refers to the elephants, who are at the center of this article.

3. Sample answer: This article explains how David Sulzer used what he observed about elephants and his knowledge of music to answer a question. *Will elephants play music?* He built huge handmade instruments and taught elephants to play them. This took place in Thailand at a conservation center, which earned money by selling albums the Thai Elephant Orchestra made.

4. Sample answer: I know that elephants like peanuts, so one meaning is that the elephants earn their pay in peanuts for working in the orchestra. But the expression of doing something "for peanuts" means to do something for very little pay.

---

16 | Summarize

Name _____ Date _____

The Man Behind Yoda

Read the biographical sketch.
Then follow the directions in the Text Marking box.

Make-up artists play an important role in movie-making. Every year, the best of them, like the best actors, directors, and screenwriters, are honored by Hollywood for their contributions. Stuart Freeborn, called by some the "grandfather of modern make-up design," may have been the best of the best.

English-born Freeborn was already famous for his imaginative work when he was hired to create characters for *Star Wars*. He'd already worked on many films and had done the make-up for scores of famous actors. This gifted artist understood faces. He knew just how to emphasize a cheekbone or arch an eyebrow.

But Stuart Freeborn is best known today for the unforgettable characters he created for the *Star Wars* movies. Fanciful creatures like Jabba the Hutt and Chewbacca were his creations. So was the tiny Jedi master, Yoda.

Yoda is odd-looking, with a pointed chin and wrinkles crossing his forehead. The resemblance between that charming pint-sized Jedi and Freeborn is unmistakable. That's because when coming up with a model for this now-famous face, Freeborn chose one he'd never used before—his own!

Stuart Freeborn worked on glamorous stars, superheroes, cavemen, and Muppets, too. He died in 2013, but his memorable characters will live on.

Stuart Freeborn with Yoda

★ **Text Marking** ★

Summarize the text.

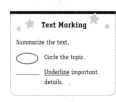

◯ Circle the topic.

___ Underline important details.

◀ Sample Text Markings

Passage 16: The Man Behind Yoda

1. D; Sample answer: In the previous paragraph, the author described Yoda as being tiny.

2. B; Sample answer: It says in paragraph 3 that Stuart Freeborn created all three.

3. Sample answer: Stuart Freeborn was a world-famous make-up artist. He worked on many movies with many actors and was highly respected. He was best known for his *Star Wars* characters, especially Yoda—whose face he modeled on his own.

4. Sample answer: A grandfather is someone older, who has been around a long time and has had many experiences, like Freeborn. But it also means that, like a grandfather, Freeborn passed on his creative techniques and brilliant make-up ideas to the generations that followed.

The Whole Bird

Read the memoir.
Then follow the directions in the Text Marking box.

No one knows who first said, "Waste not, want not," but my grandmother lived by that saying. She applied the strategy to most everything she did, especially to her cooking. Oh, what she did with chicken!

Chicken was a staple in her home, a food she served all the time. Or so it seemed to me. For dinners, she often prepared the most delicious roast chicken anyone ever ate. But that was only part of what she did with that chicken. She would use just about every part of that bird before she was done with it.

She wasted nothing, not even the extra fat, which she melted down to use in future cooking. She took out the liver and the gizzard—the bird's stomach—to save for her delicious stuffing or to flavor a meatloaf. She used the picked-over chicken carcass to make stock for soup. And, as I recall, she'd also include the bird's neck, feet, back, and wing tips for that purpose. Naturally, she used any leftover chicken meat for sandwiches, stews, or casseroles.

I try to be a smart shopper and economical cook. I don't let food go to waste. But as conscientious and frugal as I aim to be, I'll never match Grandma.

Parts of a chicken

Text Marking

Make an inference: Why does the writer admire Grandma?

_____ Underline text clues.

Think about what you already know.

Informational Passages for Text Marking & Close Reading: Grade 4
© 2015 by Scholastic Teaching Resources

◀ Sample Text Markings

Passage 17: The Whole Bird

1. D; Sample answer: In paragraph 2, *staple* is defined in the sentence as "a food she served all the time."

2. C; Sample answer: The grandmother didn't waste any part of the chicken. She used every part of the bird to stretch its value, which is a thrifty way to be.

3. Sample answer: I think the writer was inspired by how clever Grandma was in making use of every part of the foods she cooked. I think Grandma's common sense and careful habits influenced the writer's life to this day.

4. Sample answers: Maybe Grandma mended clothes to make them last longer instead of buying new ones; maybe she reused items for a long time to save money; maybe she grew her own vegetables or canned them, or baked items from scratch instead of using more expensive mixes.

Orlando Bloomed!

Read the magazine article.
Then follow the directions in the Text Marking box.

Orlando Bloom is a famous actor you may know from his roles in *The Pirates of the Caribbean* or *Lord of the Rings* films. But his life was not always so successful.

As a boy, Bloom was diagnosed with *dyslexia*, which made his school years challenging. He often felt stupid or worthless, despite his mother's steady love and support. Still, young Orlando felt anger and frustration, though he never let on to his classmates how difficult school was for him. Though he took extra classes and studied hard, his mind moved faster than his words could express. He recalls that he "had to work three times as hard to get two-thirds of the way."

He hid his problem whenever possible; he avoided reading aloud. Then Bloom discovered acting. Playing characters on stage helped him focus. Some of his fears vanished as he experienced success and respect. Through acting, Bloom was able to work around his disability, letting his creative side shine.

Bloom encourages dyslexic kids never to think they're failures, but rather to use their hurdle to find other ways to succeed. "If you can overcome this obstacle, you are going to be that much further along than anyone else," Bloom advises.

Actor Orlando Bloom

dyslexia: a learning disorder that makes reading and interpreting words very difficult

Text Marking

Make an inference: How did acting help Orlando Bloom cope with his disability?

_____ Underline text clues.

Think about what you already know.

Informational Passages for Text Marking & Close Reading: Grade 4
© 2015 by Scholastic Teaching Resources

◀ Sample Text Markings

Passage 18: Orlando Bloomed!

1. B; Sample answer: This is the only statement supported by the text. In paragraph 2 it says that having dyslexia made Bloom's school years challenging.

2. C; Sample answer: Bloom's own words in that paragraph include the word *obstacle*, and I know that an obstacle is something in your way that you must get over or around to keep going.

3. Sample answer: I think that because of his dyslexia, reading was hard for him. He probably didn't want to embarrass himself in front of his classmates or let on that he had to struggle.

4. Sample answer: According to the article, when Bloom discovered acting, it changed how he felt about himself. Being on stage playing a character helped him focus and brought out his creativity. Probably the new success and respect he earned encouraged him to keep going.

Informational Passages for Text Marking & Close Reading: Grade 4
© 2015 by Scholastic Teaching Resources

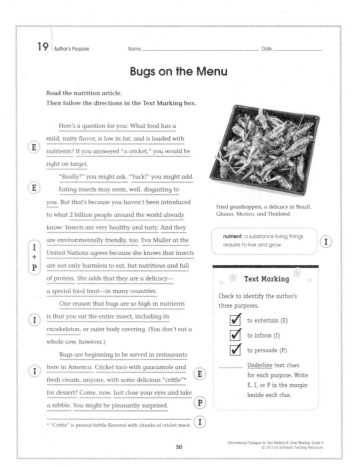

◀ Sample Text Markings

Passage 19: Bugs on the Menu

1. B; Sample answer: The context clue let me know that a *delicacy* is a special food treat. I'd be most likely to have a delicacy at a holiday party than at any of the other times described.

2. B; Sample answer: Even if this is true, the article doesn't include this information. But it does mention all the other choices.

3. Sample answer: The writer starts by asking a question whose answer is not what you'd expect. I think this is done to grab readers' attention and make them curious to know more.

4. Sample answer: The author uses a playful, funny, entertaining approach to give information about an unusual topic. It sounds like the author would be willing to try an insect meal because it is nutritious and also supports this as a good idea for the environment.

◀ Sample Text Markings

Passage 20: A Star of the Future?

1. A; Sample answer: In that paragraph, the writer refers to her skills, so I think that *feats* are accomplishments or great things that you do.

2. C; Sample answer: The writer says that the more opportunities girls get to play against boys, the more the girls will show that they can be "equal to the task."

3. Sample answer: The author admits that Mo'ne is amazing as a 13-year-old Little League player, but doubts whether her skills will be able to keep up with the skills that boys typically develop as they grow.

4. Sample answer: Although the writer argues that Mo'ne is unlikely to succeed as a young female competing against young male ballplayers, it sounds like the writer holds out hope that she just might.

Informational Passages for Text Marking & Close Reading: Grade 4
© 2015 by Scholastic Teaching Resources

Notes

Informational Passages for Text Marking & Close Reading: Grade 4
© 2015 by Scholastic Teaching Resources